DATE DUE			

LET'S INVESTIGATE
Quadrilaterals

LET'S INVESTIGATE
Quadrilaterals

By Marion Smoothey

Illustrated by Ted Evans

MARSHALL CAVENDISH
NEW YORK · LONDON · TORONTO · SYDNEY

Library Edition Published 1993

Published by Marshall Cavendish Corporation
2415 Jerusalem Avenue
PO Box 587
North Bellmore
New York 11710

Series created by Graham Beehag Book Design

Library of Congress Cataloging-in-Publication Data

Smoothey, Marion, 1943-
    Quadrilaterals / by Marion Smoothey; illustrated by Ted Evans.
       p. cm.. -- (Let's Investigate)
    Includes index.
    Summary: Introduces quadrilaterals, which are closed shapes made up of four straight lines, through a combination of theory and problems.
    ISBN 1-85435-459-0 ISBN 1-85435-455-8 (set)
    1. Quadrilaterals -- Juvenile literature. [1. Quadrilaterals]
    I. Evans, Ted ill. II. Title. III. Series: Smoothey, Marion, 1943-
    Let's Investigate.
    QA482.S66 1992   92-10436
    516'.15---dc20   CIP
                                           AC

Printed in Singapore by Times Offset PTE Ltd
Bound in the United States

Contents

What are Quadrilaterals?

On a large piece of scrap paper, draw four dots in any position you like. Number them from 1 to 4 in a clockwise direction.

Join the numbers as shown below, in order, 1 to 2, 2 to 3 and so on, with straight lines.

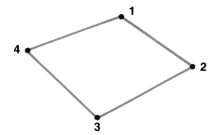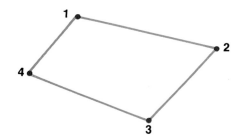

Repeat, for as many different ways of arranging the dots as you can think of.

● What is the same about all the shapes that you have drawn?

8

All the shapes you made by joining four dots with straight lines, in a clockwise order, resulted in closed shapes with four straight lines. A closed shape is one with no gaps in its outside edge.

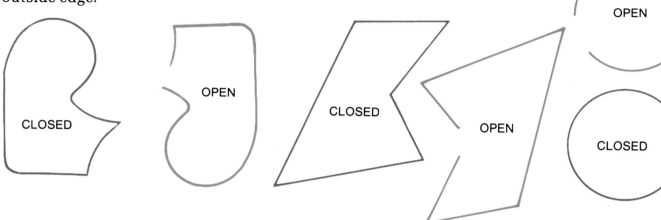

They are all quadrilaterals A quadrilateral is any closed shape made up of four straight lines.
● Which of the shapes below are quadrilaterals?

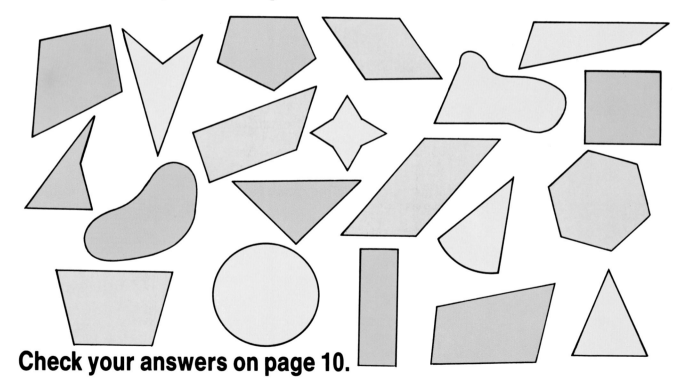

Check your answers on page 10.

Investigating Dots and Quadrilaterals

9

You need dotted paper. You can make some, if necessary, by marking dots at the corners of graph paper squares.

● Use nine dots at a time. See how many different quadrilaterals you can make, by joining any of the dots with straight lines. Here are three shapes to get you started.

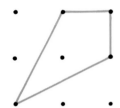 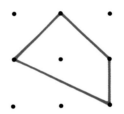 

These do not count as different. They are all the same quadrilateral in different positions.

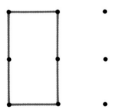 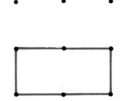 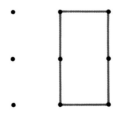 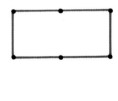

These all count as one also.

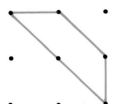 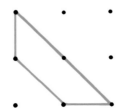 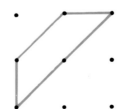 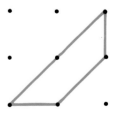

Answers to page 8
These are the quadrilaterals.

10

If you were correct, turn to page 9.

If you made mistakes, identify the quadrilaterals in the group of figures below.

Turn to page 12.

Parallel Lines

Parallel lines always remain the same distance apart from each other. They will never meet, however far you extend them. Railway tracks are made up of parallel rails. Any number of lines may be parallel to each other.

◇ Look at how many sets of parallel lines there are on this construction site. Look around you and see how many sets of parallel lines you can spot.

Parallel

Not Parallel

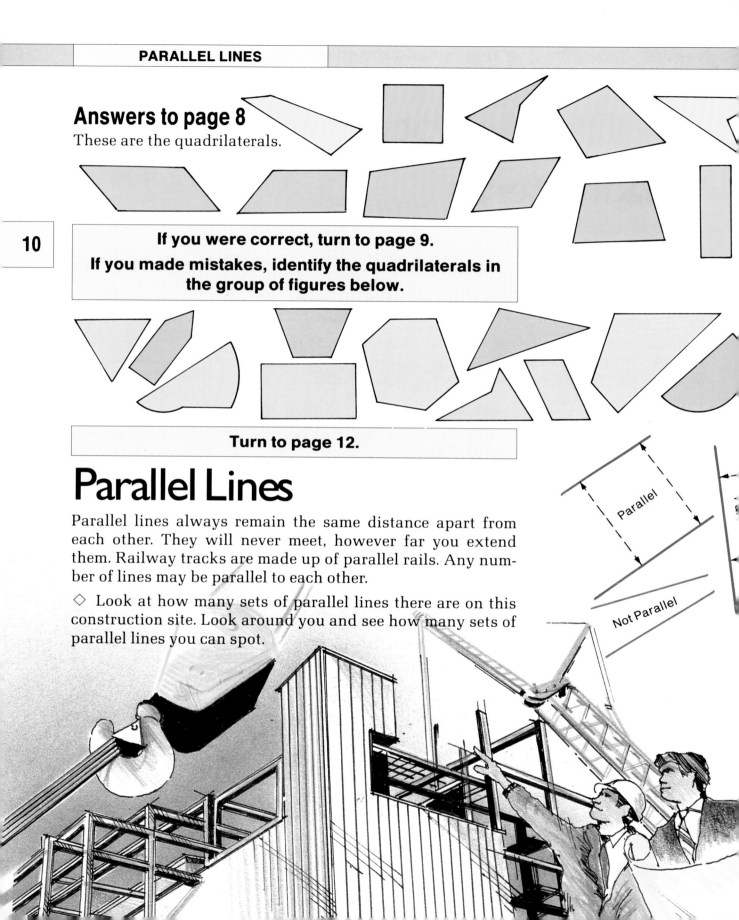

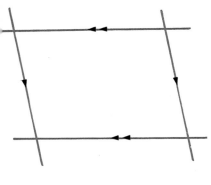

In mathematical diagrams, matching pairs of arrows are used to show that a set of lines are parallel.

The Names of some Special Quadrilaterals

Some quadrilaterals can be grouped together because they share particular properties. These special quadrilaterals have names to identify them.

Parallelograms

A **parallelogram** has two pairs of parallel sides.

In a parallelogram the shortest distance between a pair of sides is the same wherever you measure it. With a ruler, measure these diagrams of parallelograms to see if this is true.

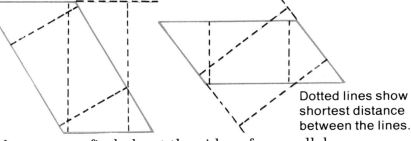

Dotted lines show shortest distance between the lines.

● What else can you find about the sides of a parallelogram, using your ruler?

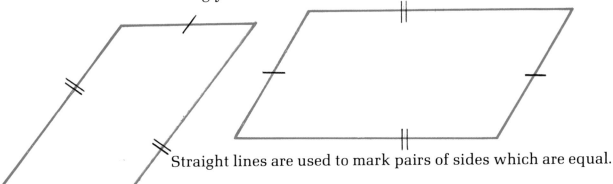

Straight lines are used to mark pairs of sides which are equal.

Rectangles

A **rectangle** is a parallelogram which has four **right angles**, angles of 90 degrees.

Right angles

Rectangles

● How many rectangles can you see around you now?

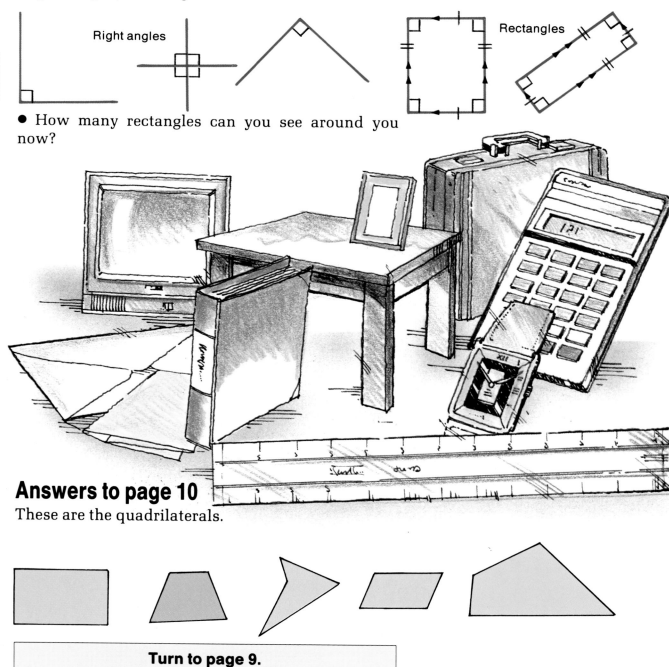

Answers to page 10

These are the quadrilaterals.

Turn to page 9.

ombuses

ombus is a parallelogram
equal sides.

Squares

A **square** is a rectangle with equal sides.

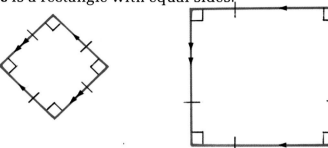

Kites

A **kite** is a quadrilateral with two pairs of equal sides and one pair of equal angles.

Arrowheads

An **arrowhead** is also a quadrilateral with two pairs of equal sides and one pair of equal angles. A kite and an arrowhead look like their names.

Trapezia

A **trapezoid** has one pair of parallel lines.

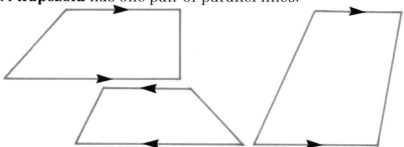

14

Answers to dots and quadrilaterals – page 9

Here are some possibilities. You may have found others, but make sure they are really different and not just moved around the grid. Also make sure they only have four sides!

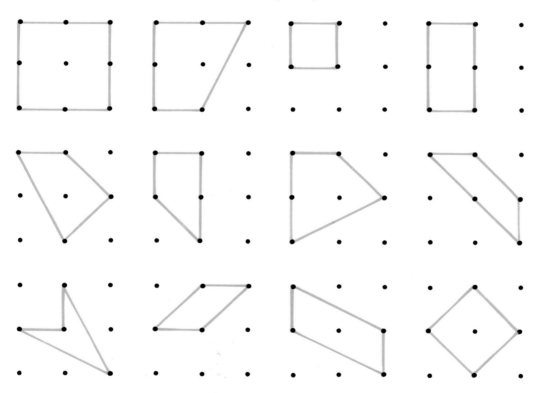

You should now be able to give the correct names to all the quadrilaterals on the grids.

Quadrilateral Word Search

● Copy this word search. Do not write on the book. In it are hidden thirteen words related to quadrilaterals. They may be read forward or backward, in a straight line, in any direction.

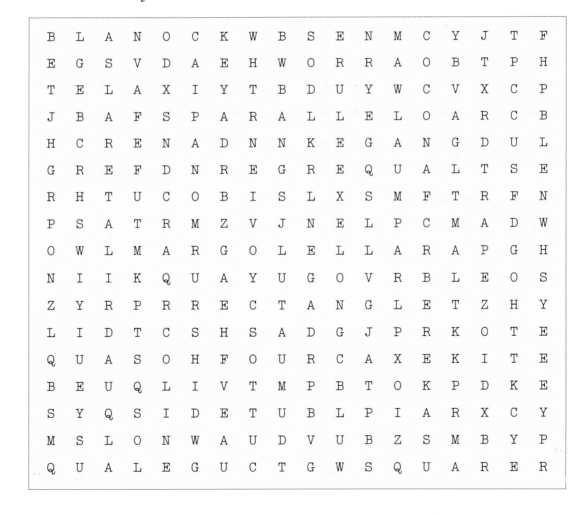

```
B  L  A  N  O  C  K  W  B  S  E  N  M  C  Y  J  T  F
E  G  S  V  D  A  E  H  W  O  R  R  A  O  B  T  P  H
T  E  L  A  X  I  Y  T  B  D  U  Y  W  C  V  X  C  P
J  B  A  F  S  P  A  R  A  L  L  E  L  O  A  R  C  B
H  C  R  E  N  A  D  N  N  K  E  G  A  N  G  D  U  L
G  R  E  F  D  N  R  E  G  R  E  Q  U  A  L  T  S  E
R  H  T  U  C  O  B  I  S  L  X  S  M  F  T  R  F  N
P  S  A  T  R  M  Z  V  J  N  E  L  P  C  M  A  D  W
O  W  L  M  A  R  G  O  L  E  L  L  A  R  A  P  G  H
N  I  I  K  Q  U  A  Y  U  G  O  V  R  B  L  E  O  S
Z  Y  R  P  R  R  E  C  T  A  N  G  L  E  T  Z  H  Y
L  I  D  T  C  S  H  S  A  D  G  J  P  R  K  O  T  E
Q  U  A  S  O  H  F  O  U  R  C  A  X  E  K  I  T  E
B  E  U  Q  L  I  V  T  M  P  B  T  O  K  P  D  K  E
S  Y  Q  S  I  D  E  T  U  B  L  P  I  A  R  X  C  Y
M  S  L  O  N  W  A  U  D  V  U  B  Z  S  M  B  Y  P
Q  U  A  L  E  G  U  C  T  G  W  S  Q  U  A  R  E  R
```

Answers to sorting and naming the quadrilaterals on page 14

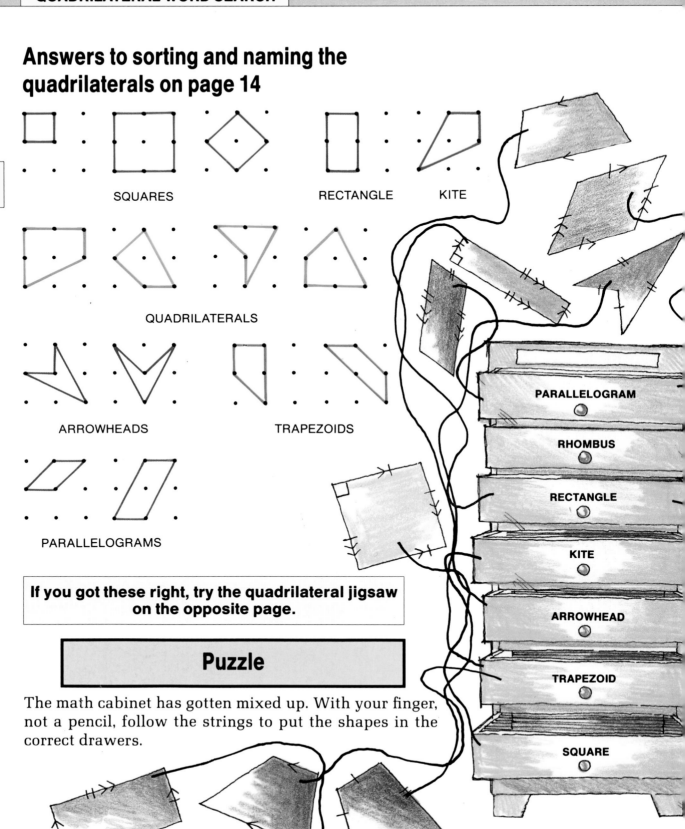

SQUARES

RECTANGLE

KITE

QUADRILATERALS

ARROWHEADS

TRAPEZOIDS

PARALLELOGRAMS

PARALLELOGRAM

RHOMBUS

RECTANGLE

KITE

ARROWHEAD

TRAPEZOID

SQUARE

If you got these right, try the quadrilateral jigsaw on the opposite page.

Puzzle

The math cabinet has gotten mixed up. With your finger, not a pencil, follow the strings to put the shapes in the correct drawers.

Quadrilateral Jigsaw

● Copy these quadrilaterals *accurately* onto thick paper or thin cardboard. Cut them out carefully. Time yourself to see how long it takes you to rearrange them to exactly fill a rectangle $5\frac{1}{4}''$ long and $4''$ tall.

17

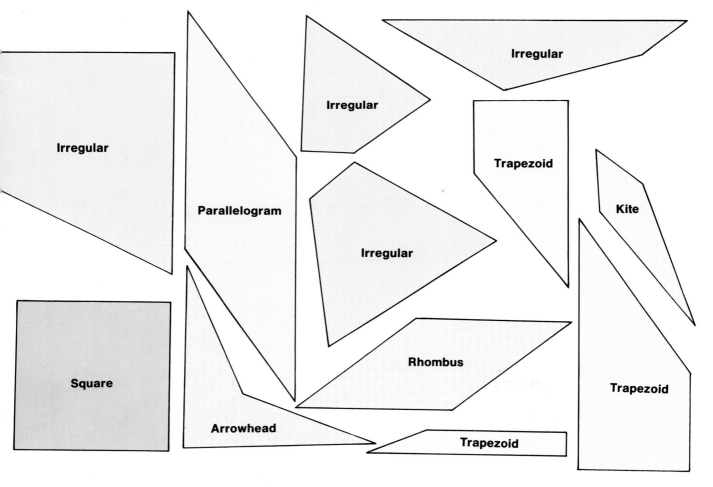

Irregular

Irregular

Irregular

Parallelogram

Trapezoid

Kite

Irregular

Square

Rhombus

Trapezoid

Arrowhead

Trapezoid

Trapezoid

☆ **Hints**

It is a good idea to draw the rectangle to fit the pieces into.

The parallelogram, arrowhead, rhombus and kite all touch the square.

Folds, Cuts and Quadrilaterals

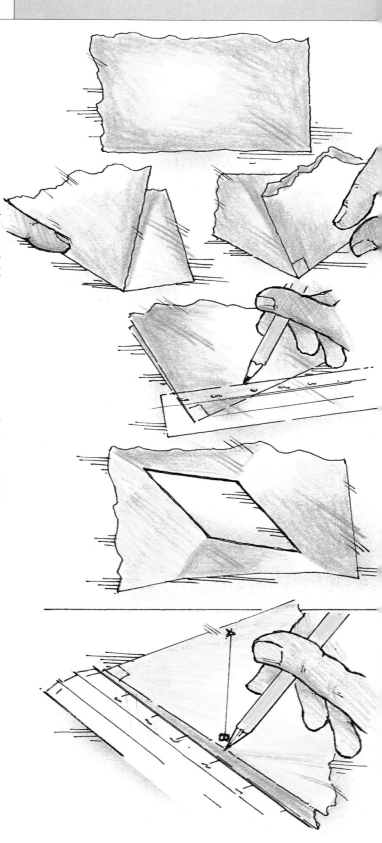

18

You need plenty of scrap paper. Old newspaper will do.

1. Fold a piece of paper. Fold the fold over on itself again to make a right angle.

Draw a line as shown and cut along it.
● Open up the piece shaded in the diagram. Follow the flow chart on the opposite page to identify it.

2. Take a second piece of paper. Fold it as before. Mark two points, A and B, at equal distances from the corner fold. Join A and B with a straight line.

◇ What shape do you think the cut piece will be when it is unfolded?

Cut it and unfold it. Were you right?

● **3.** Can you make a square from a rectangle, with one fold and one cut?

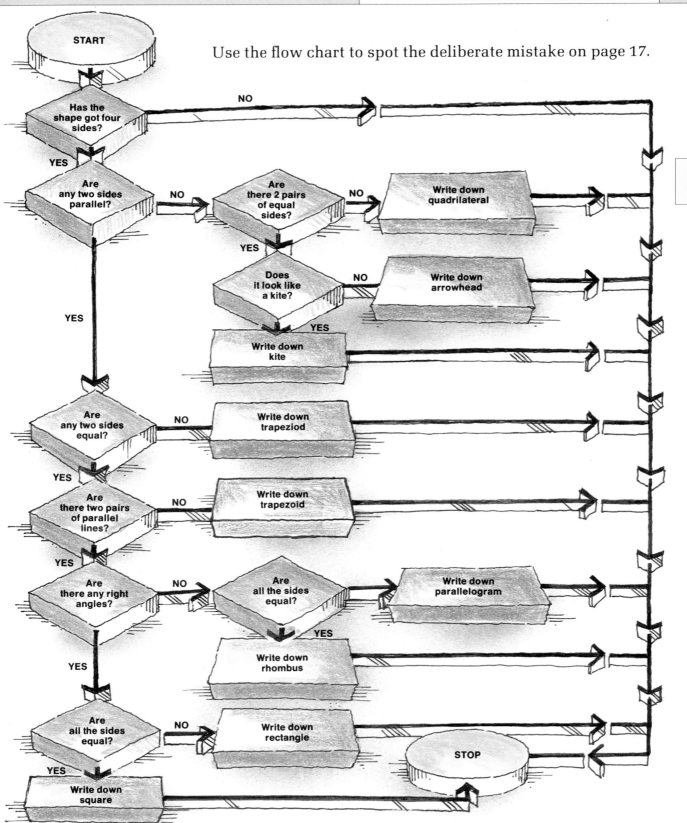

Use the flow chart to spot the deliberate mistake on page 17.

START

Has the shape got four sides?
NO

YES

Are any two sides parallel?
NO

Are there 2 pairs of equal sides?
NO
Write down quadrilateral

YES

Does it look like a kite?
NO
Write down arrowhead

YES
Write down kite

YES

Are any two sides equal?
NO
Write down trapeziod

YES

Are there two pairs of parallel lines?
NO
Write down trapezoid

YES

Are there any right angles?
NO

Are all the sides equal?
Write down parallelogram

YES
Write down rhombus

YES

Are all the sides equal?
NO
Write down rectangle

STOP

YES

Write down square

Quadrilateral jigsaw– how did you rate?

Less than five minutes – Amazing!
Five to ten minutes – Excellent
Ten to twenty minutes – Well done
Over twenty minutes – Full marks for perseverance
Gave up? – Try again, starting like this.

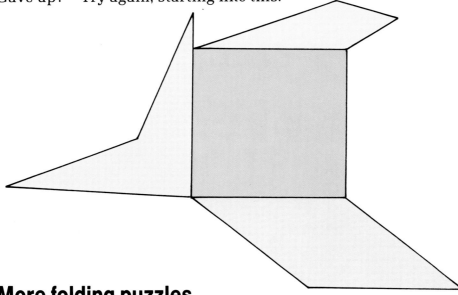

More folding puzzles

4. Make a square. Use two folds to find the center. Open up the square. Fold each corner to the center.

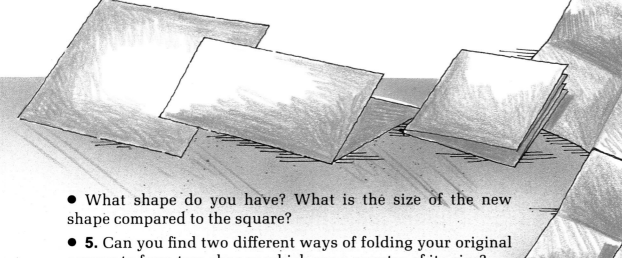

● What shape do you have? What is the size of the new shape compared to the square?

● **5.** Can you find two different ways of folding your original square to form two shapes which are a quarter of its size?

Tricky Squares with Matchsticks!

● **1.** Remove four matchsticks to leave nine squares.

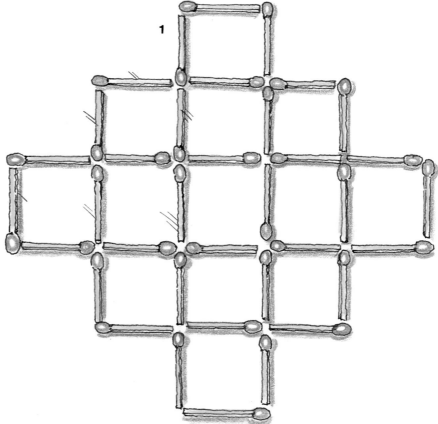

● **2.** Move two matchsticks to make seven squares.

● **3.** Start with the same pattern as **2.** Remove four matchsticks to leave two squares.

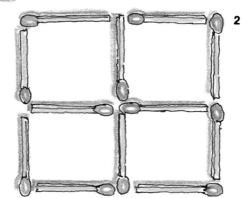

Answers to folding puzzles

1. The shape is called a **rhombus**. It is like a square which has been pushed over.

2. The shape is a square.

3. Fold a side to meet the top or bottom. Cut off the single strip of paper which remains on the other side.

4. The new shape is another square which is half the size of the first square.

22

5. The two shapes are a square and a triangle.

These diagrams show that the new shapes are a quarter of the original square.

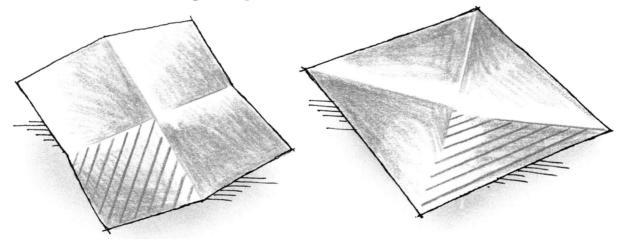

● How can you make a square twice as big as this one by moving two of the dots?

Drawing Quadrilaterals

24

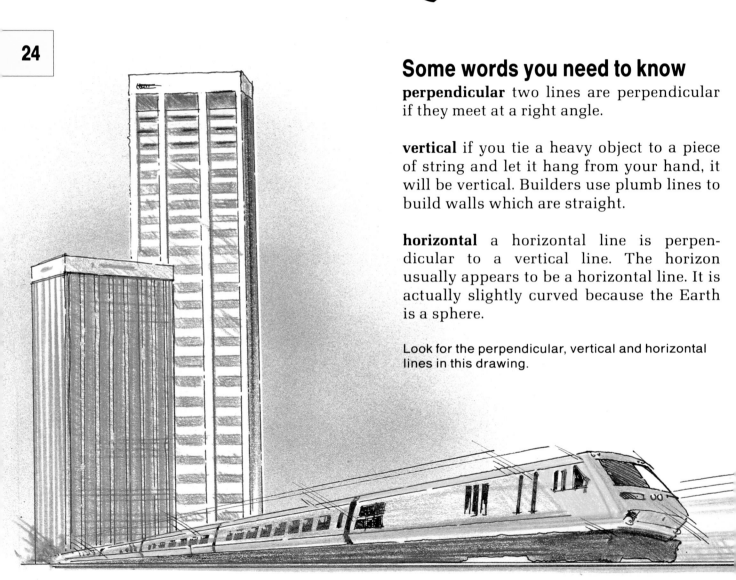

Some words you need to know

perpendicular two lines are perpendicular if they meet at a right angle.

vertical if you tie a heavy object to a piece of string and let it hang from your hand, it will be vertical. Builders use plumb lines to build walls which are straight.

horizontal a horizontal line is perpendicular to a vertical line. The horizon usually appears to be a horizontal line. It is actually slightly curved because the Earth is a sphere.

Look for the perpendicular, vertical and horizontal lines in this drawing.

◇ Look around the room and count how many horizontal, vertical and perpendicular lines you can see.

☆ **DRAW THE FOLLOWING QUADRILATERALS ON SCRAP PAPER. YOU WILL NEED TO CUT AND FOLD THEM LATER.**

Drawing squares and rectangles

The easiest way to draw a square is to use a set square.

To draw a square with 3″ sides.

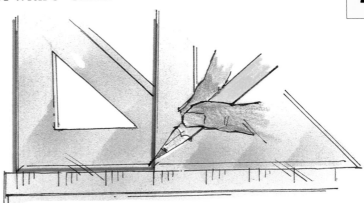

1. Leave enough space for your square and draw a line. Measure off 3″

2. Use your set square to draw a **vertical line** 3″ long. Move the set square to the other mark on the line and draw another vertical line 3″ long.

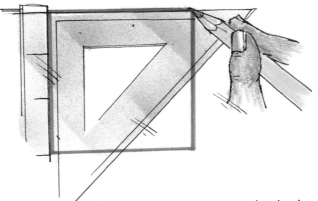

3. Use your set square as a check when you draw the final side.

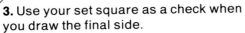

Drawing a square with compass and ruler

Use your compass to mark the line with two points **A** and **B** 3″ apart.

Decrease the distance between the point of the compass and the pencil. Place the point of the compass at **A** and draw two arcs, one each side. Repeat for **B**.

Place the point of the compass on one of the arcs which you have just drawn and make a new arc above the line. Repeat for the other three arcs. This gives you two pairs of intersecting arcs which show you where the sides of the square need to be drawn.

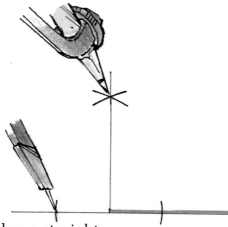

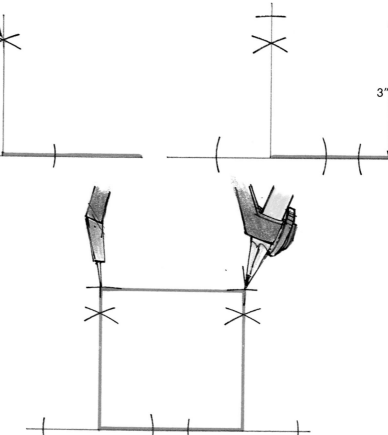

With a ruler, draw straight lines from the ends of the base line through the intersecting arcs. Mark off 3″ along these lines with your compass. Put the point of the compass on the 3″ marks and draw arcs on the opposite sides. Join up the final side of the square where the last two pairs of arcs intersect.

◇ Make yourself a perpendicular (90°) tester as shown on page 18 in step **1**. Check that the four angles of your square are right angles.

Drawing rectangles

You can easily adapt the methods of drawing a square to construct rectangles. You follow the same steps but make the appropiate changes in the length of sides.

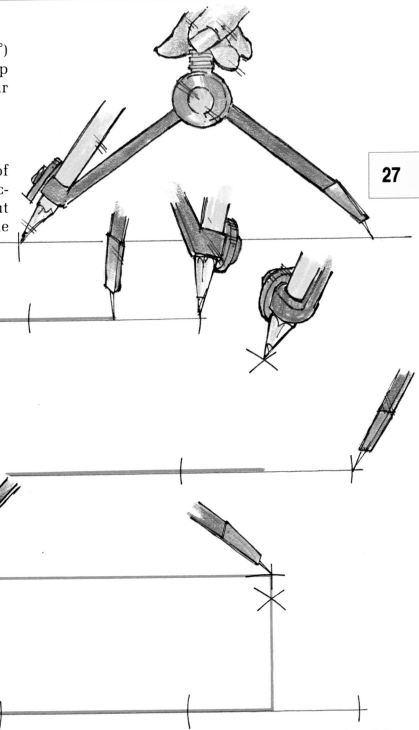

◇ Draw a rectangle $2\frac{1}{2}''$ long and $1\frac{1}{2}''$ wide.

Drawing parallelograms, rhombuses and trapezia

You can use a set square or a compass to draw sets of parallel lines.

28

Drawing parallel lines with a set square and ruler

Draw a line. Place the set square along the line, and the ruler along one of the other edges of the set square.

Slide the set square up or down, keeping the edge against the ruler. You can draw as many lines as you like. They will all be parallel to the original line.

You can slide the set square up and down the rule to draw as many parallel lines as you wish.

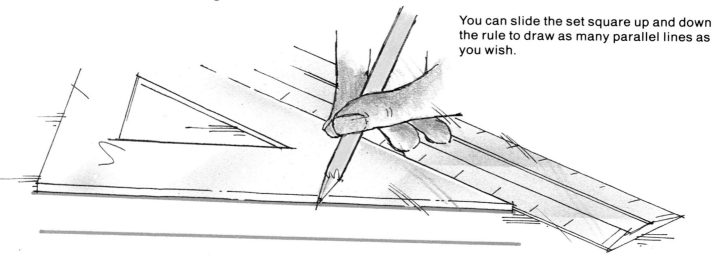

Drawing parallel lines with a compass

Draw a line. Mark two points on it. Set your compass to $1\frac{1}{4}''$. Place the compass point on each mark in turn and draw an arc.

Place a ruler so that each arc touches it at only one point. Draw a line. The new line is parallel to the original line and $1\frac{1}{4}''$ away from it.

Make sure the ruler touches both arcs at only one point.

Mark off the distance you require on the line. Slide the set square up or down the ruler to make the parallel lines where you need them.

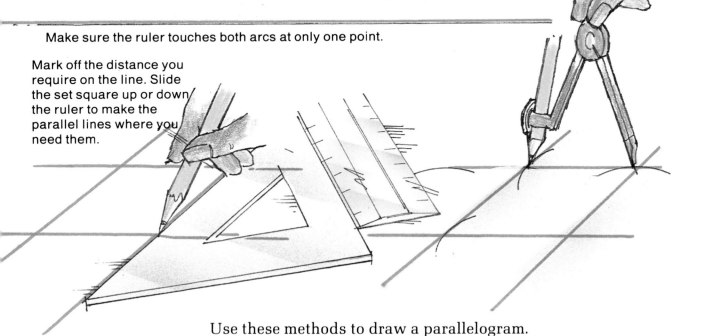

Use these methods to draw a parallelogram.

◇ Use compass, protractor, ruler and pencil to draw this parallelogram.

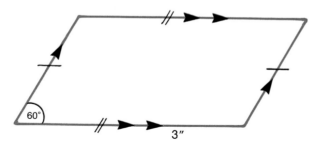

◇ Draw a rhombus with 3″ sides, using only compass, ruler and pencil.

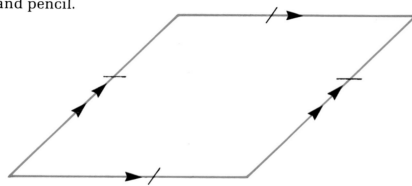

● Draw a trapezoid with sides of the indicated lengths. What is the length of side **x**?

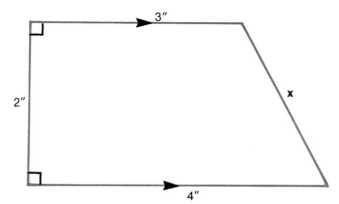

Drawing kites and arrowheads

1. Mark two points **A** and **B**.

2. Place your compass point at **B** and draw two arcs equidistant from **B**.

3. Change the distance between the pencil and compass point. Place the compass point on **A** and draw two equidistant arcs.

4. Draw four lines to join **A** and **B** to the points of intersection of the arcs.

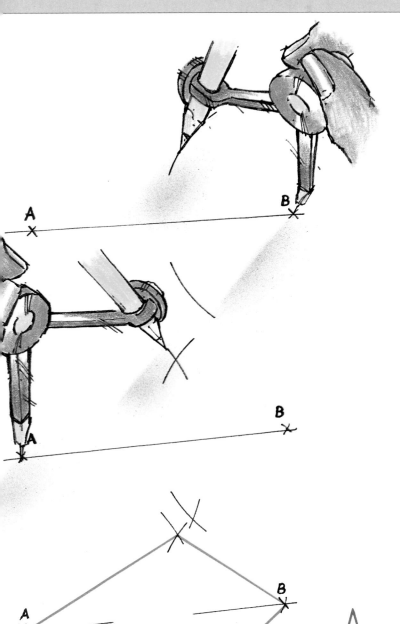

◇ Draw this kite. Measure angle **a**.

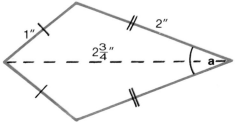

In the flow chart on page 17 the rhombus was identified as a parallelogram with four equal sides. It can also be thought of as a kite with four equal sides.

● How do you need to adapt the method for drawing a kite in order to draw this arrowhead?

Investigating Straws and Quadrilaterals

32

Cut drinking straws so that you have two lengths of 3″, two of 4″, two of 5″ and one of 6″. If you can use different colored straws for each length, it makes recording your results easier.

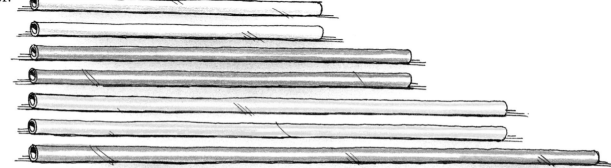

● **1.** How many rectangles can you make using all or some of the straws? Decide on a way to record all the possibilities.

You might decide to record this rectangle as BYBY.

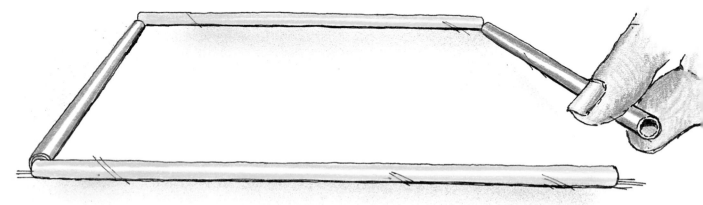

● **2.** How many possible squares are there?

● **3.** and **4.** Can you say how many parallelograms and rhombuses can be made by looking at your results for **1.** and **2.**?

● **5.** and **6.** How many kites and arrowheads can you make?

Check your drawings

If two shapes are **congruent**, they are exactly the same size and shape. One should fit exactly on top of the other.

◇ Cut out your square from page 26 and your rectangle from page 27. Make sure they are **congruent** with the drawings below.

33

The parallelogram which you drew on page 30 should be **congruent** with this one.

◇ Check it by placing it on top of the drawing.

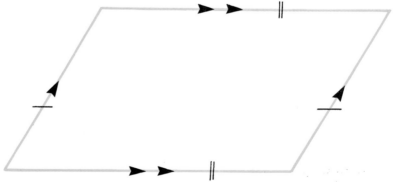

◇ If your shapes are not congruent with the ones in the book, try drawing them again.

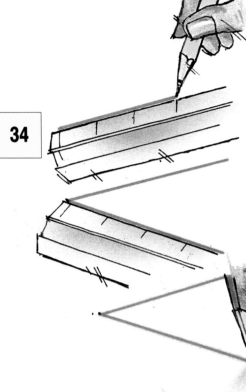

34

Two ways of constructing a rhombus with 3 inch sides using a compass

1. As a parallelogram of equal sides.

a) Draw a line 3″ long. From one end of it, draw another line 3″ long.

b) Measure off 3″ with the compass. Place the point of the compass at the end of one of the lines and draw an arc.

c) Repeat for the end of the other line.

d) Draw lines to the point of intersection of the arcs to form the rhombus.

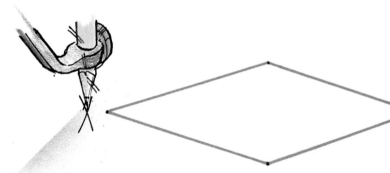

2. As a kite of equal sides

a) Draw a line of any length less than 6″. Set the compass to 3″. Place the compass point at one end of the line and draw two arcs.

b) Repeat for the other end of the line.

c) Draw four lines from the ends of the lines to the points of intersection of the arcs. This will form a rhombus with 3″ sides.

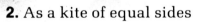

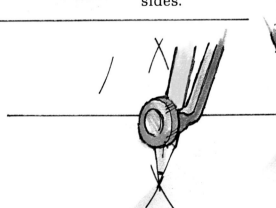

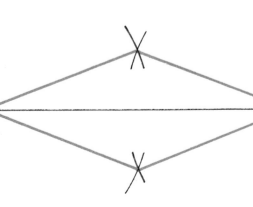

There are an infinite number of rhombuses with 3″ sides. Remember that a rhombus is like a "pushed over" square; you can push it over a tiny bit or a lot. These rhombuses are both have the same length sides.

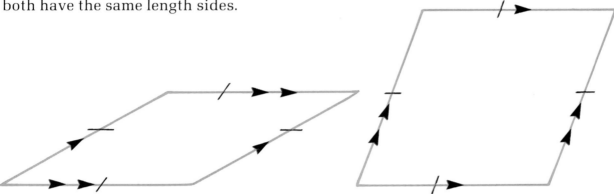

Check that each of the sides of your rhombus measures 3″

The length **x** of the side of the trapezoid which you drew on page 30 should be $2\frac{1}{4}$″. Cut out your trapezoid and check that it is congruent with this one.

Your kite drawing from page 31 should be congruent with this one. Angle **a** is 32 degrees.

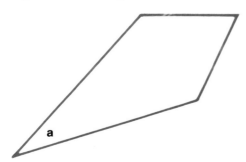

How to draw an arrowhead instead of a kite

When you draw the arcs from the end of the line, draw them
beyond the line instead of between the two ends.

Make a drawing to match this one.

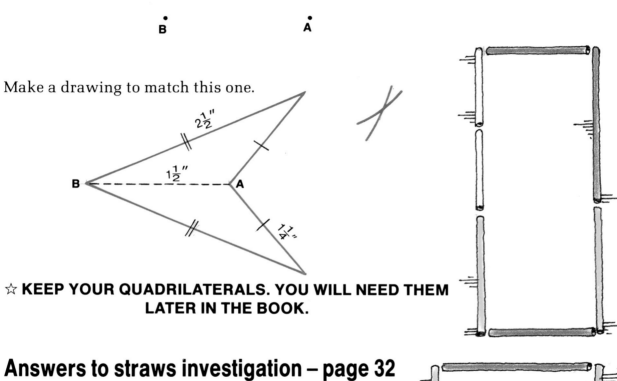

☆ **KEEP YOUR QUADRILATERALS. YOU WILL NEED THEM
LATER IN THE BOOK.**

Answers to straws investigation – page 32

1. You can make seven rectangles.

2. There are no squares.

3. and **4.** There are seven main groups of parallelograms which match the seven rectangles, because parallelograms are like "pushed over" rectangles. There are actually an infinite number of parallelograms depending on how far over you "push" each rectangle.

If you do not believe this, cut two 3″ and two 5″ strips of cardboard. These match your white and yellow straws. With a hole punch, make a hole at each end of each strip. Try to position the hole the same distance away from the end of the strip in each case. Join the strip with paper fasteners, or bent paper clips, to make a rectangle. You can now push over the rectangle to make many different parallelograms.

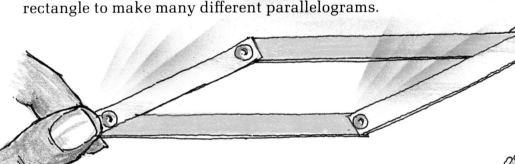

There are no rhombuses because there are no squares.

5. and **6.** All the rectangles can be rearranged as kites and arrowheads. Each group of these can be "stretched" long and thin or short and wide like the parallelograms.

Scores
All correct – Super smart
About $\frac{3}{4}$ correct – You're getting the hang of quadrilaterals
About $\frac{1}{2}$ correct – Look carefully at the ones you missed

Just One Cut

Each of the shapes **1** to **9** were squares. They have been cut and rearranged. You can see how this one was done.

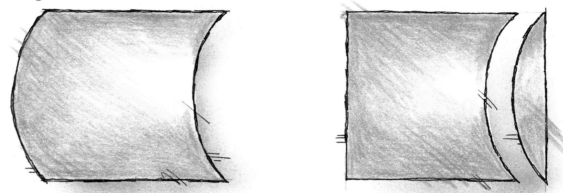

Just one cut will enable you to reform the square in each example. You may be able to see the necessary cut in your imagination, or you may need to trace the shapes and use scissors.

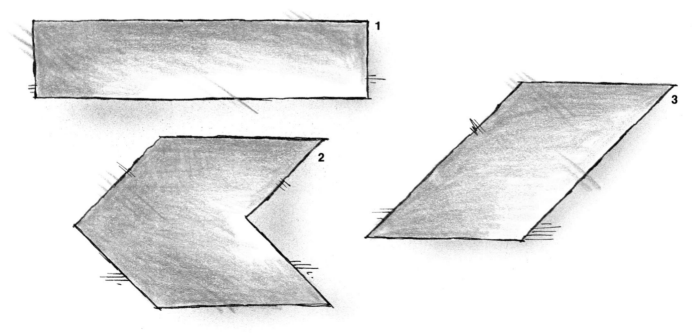

The completed quadrilateral jigsaw from page 17

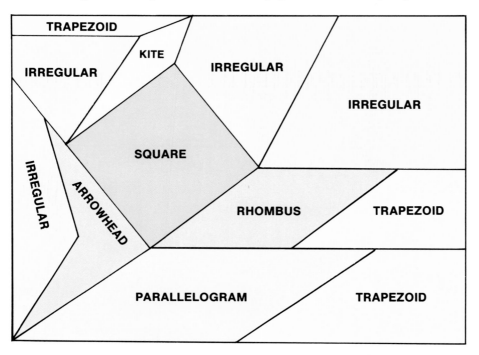

TRAPEZOID

KITE

IRREGULAR

IRREGULAR

IRREGULAR

IRREGULAR

SQUARE

ARROWHEAD

RHOMBUS

TRAPEZOID

PARALLELOGRAM

TRAPEZOID

Answers to Tricky Squares with matchsticks from page 21

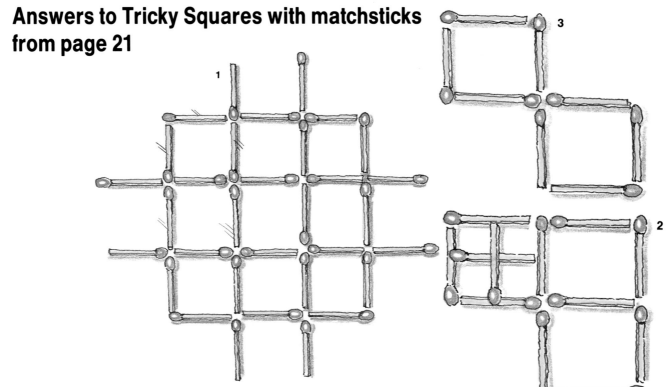

40

Diagonals and Quadrilaterals

 YOU NEED THE QUADRILATERALS YOU CONSTRUCTED FOR PAGES 25 TO 31.

Words you need to know

Diagonals

If you take a square A B C D and fold corner B on to corner D the fold line is a **diagonal**. You can also draw the diagonals with a ruler.

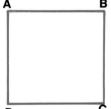 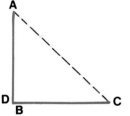 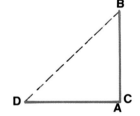 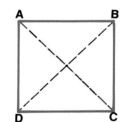

Bisect

To **bisect** means to cut in half. You can bisect an angle or a line.

Vertex

The **vertices** of a quadrilateral are the points at which the sides meet. You might call them corners, but we usually think of the two sides of a corner as making a right angle, and this is not always the case with the vertices of a quadrilateral.

Points **A B C D** are the vertices of this quadrilateral.

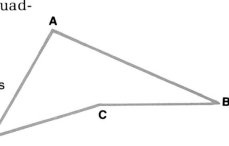

Label the vertices of each of your quadrilaterals. You should have a square, a rectangle, a parallelogram, a rhombus, a kite, an arrowhead and a trapezium.

It does not matter at which vertex you start, but it is important that you keep going around in the same direction.

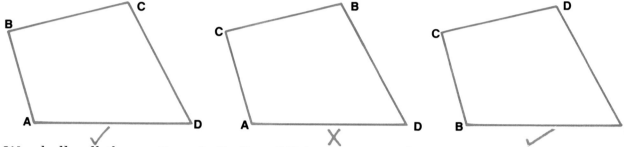

We shall call the vertices A, B, C and D but you can choose any letters to label a quadrilateral. People usually choose letters which run in alphabetical order and write them as capital letters.

Mark the diagonals on each of your quadrilaterals. You can do this by folding or by drawing lines with a ruler. Remember, you join A to C and B to D. The diagonals of an arrowhead can only intersect outside it.

Copy this table. Use your quadrilaterals to answer Yes or No in each space. You can answer most of the questions by folding. You also need a ruler and your perpendicular tester or a set square.

	Do the diagonals bisect each other	Are the diagonals equal?	Are the diagonals perpendicular to each other?	Do the diagonals bisect the angles at the vertices?
Square				
Rectangle				
Parallelogram				
Rhombus				
Kite				
Arrowhead				
Trapezoid (not isosceles)				

Answers to square puzzles on pages 38 to 39

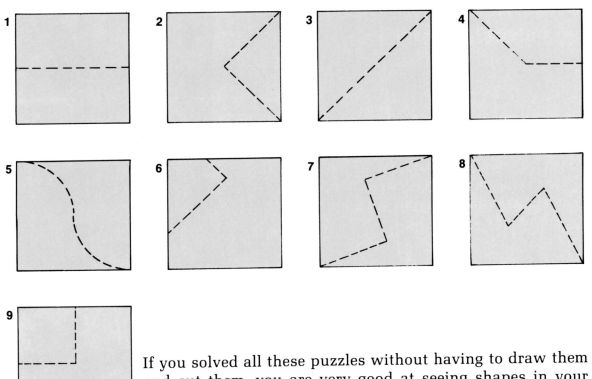

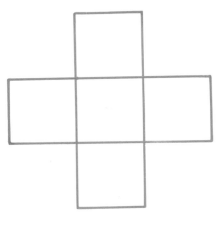

If you solved all these puzzles without having to draw them and cut them, you are very good at seeing shapes in your mind's eye.

If you solved them all by cutting in less than a quarter of an hour, that is still excellent.

It is much easier to make these puzzles than to solve them. You might like to make some to try out on your friends.

More squares to puzzle over

This shape, made from five equal squares joined together, is called a Greek Cross. It can be cut into five pieces and re-arranged to make one square. How?

Angles in Quadrilaterals

A reminder about angles

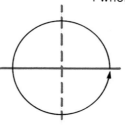

¼ turn = 90°

½ turn = 180°

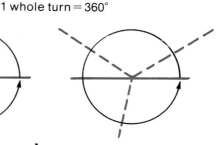

1 whole turn = 360°

On a piece of scrap paper, draw three different **irregular** quadrilaterals. An irregular quadrilateral is not one of the special quadrilaterals which you have learned to identify on pages 11-14.

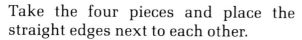

Cut out the first quadrilateral which you have just drawn, and tear off the corners.

Take the four pieces and place the straight edges next to each other.

● What do you notice about the angle at the point where the four pieces meet?

Repeat for the other two quadrilaterals.

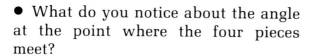

◇ Try the same experiment with all the special quadrilaterals you drew.

● How many degrees do the four angles of a quadrilateral add up to?

Find the missing angles

Use what you know about the sum of angles in a quadrilateral to find the missing angles. Do not use a protractor.

45

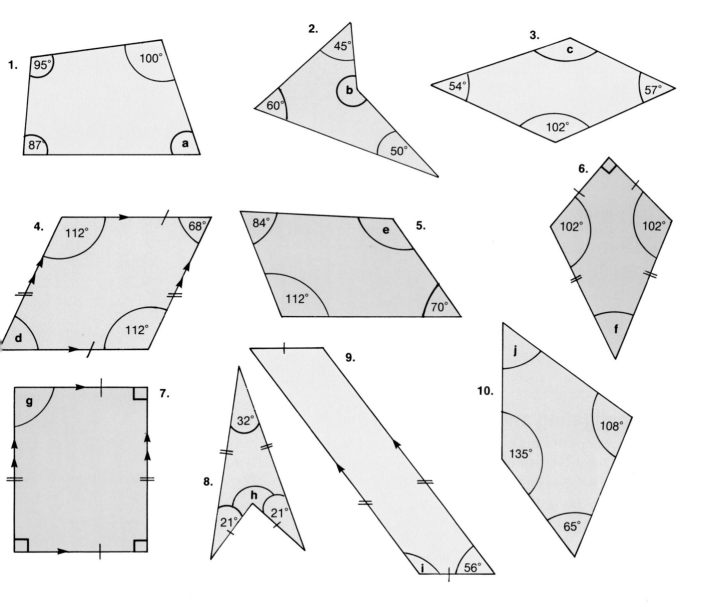

Another way of looking at the sum of angles in a quadrilateral

When you investigated diagonals and quadrilaterals (pages 41-42), you found that every quadrilateral can be divided into two triangles by drawing a diagonal.

It can be proved that the sum of the angles in any triangle is 180 degrees. Because a quadrilateral is made up of two triangles joined together, the sum of the angles of a quadrilateral must be $2 \times 180 = 360$ degrees.

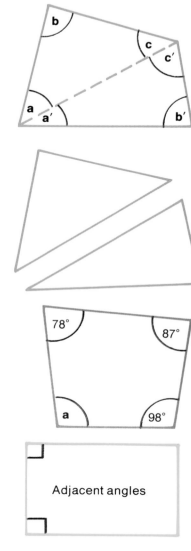

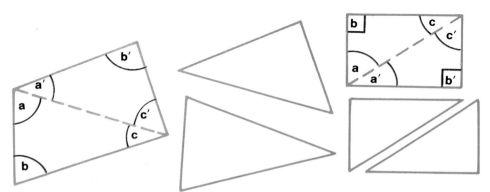

You can use the fact that the sum of the angles in any quadrilateral is 360 degrees to calculate the fourth angle of a quadrilateral when you know the other three.

In the diagram right the three marked angles add up to 263 degrees.

$78 + 87 + 98 = 263$

Therefore angle **a** must equal $360 - 263$, which is 97 degrees.

This is the method you should have used to find the angles in the quadrilaterals on the previous page.

Investigating angles in special quadrilaterals

On scrap paper make accurate drawings of a square, a rhombus, a parallelogram, a rectangle, a kite, an arrowhead and a trapezoid. Cut them out carefully.

Make a copy of the table on the opposite page. By folding, or by measuring with a protractor, fill in the table. Two entries are already made to get you started.

Adjacent angles

Opposite angles

	Are opposite angles equal?	Are adjacent angles equal?	Are all angles equal?
Square			
Parallelogram			No
Rectangle			
Kite			
Arrowhead			
Trapezium		Usually no	

An isosceles trapezoid

A trapezoid in which the non-parallel sides are equal is called an isosceles trapezoid.

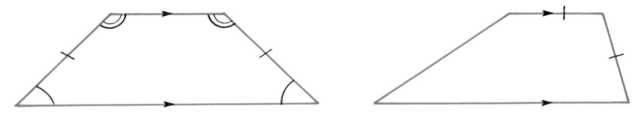

An isosceles trapezoid is the only kind of trapezoid which has two pairs of adjacent equal angles.

Puzzle

● What do you call a trapezoid with the parallel sides equal?

What Am I?

● **1.** Draw two different sized circles which intersect. With four straight lines, join each center to each point of intersection. What is the name of the shape you have drawn?

● **2.** Draw two circles of the same size which intersect. Join their centers to the points of intersection. What shape do you get this time?

All Square

A game for two or more players.

You need a $2\frac{1}{2}$" square piece of square dotted paper. Each player needs a different colored pen or pencil.

The object of the game is to complete the highest number of squares.

Each player in turn joins two dots to make one side of a square. The player who draws the fourth line of a square claims it and writes his or her initial in it. That player then has another turn. If the player completes another square, he or she claims it and has another turn. When the player does not complete a square, the turn passes to the next player.

When the whole grid is completed, the players count up their squares to see who has won.

Angles and Parallel Lines

Vertically opposite angles

Consider two straight lines which intersect and the angles **a** and **a'**.

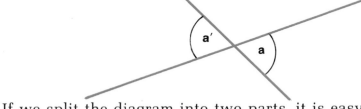

If we split the diagram into two parts, it is easy to see that **a** + **b** = 180 (half a turn, the angles on a straight line) and so does **a'** + **b** for the same reason.

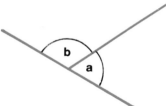 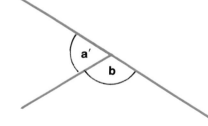

● What does that prove about **a** and **a'**?

Alternate angles

When a straight line crosses a pair of parallel lines it forms a pair of alternate or Z angles.

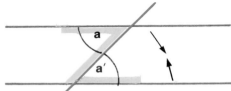

If you imagine pushing the parallel lines together until they meet, the alternate angles become vertically opposite angles.

● What does this prove about Z angles?

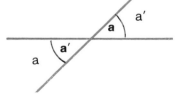

Corresponding angles

Corresponding angles also occur when a straight line intersects with a pair of parallel lines.

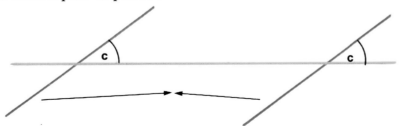

● Imagine moving the two parallel lines toward each other until they become one. What does this tell you about corresponding angles?

Alternate angles are equal · Corresponding angles are equal

Another look at angles in quadrilaterals

You should have gotten results like these when you investigated angles in special quadrilaterals on pages 46 and 47.

	Are opposite angles equal?	Are adjacent angles equal?	Are all angles equal?
Square	Yes	Yes	Yes
Rhombus	Yes	No	No
Parallelogram	Yes	No	No
Rectangle	Yes	Yes	Yes
Kite	Only one pair	No	No
Arrowhead	Only one pair	No	No
Trapezoid	No	Usually no	No

Now that you know about corresponding and alternate angles, you should be able to see why these results must be correct.

50

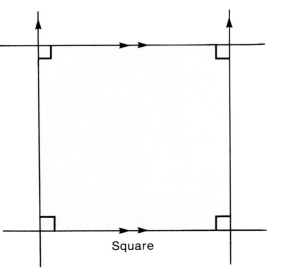

Square

All the angles are right angles.

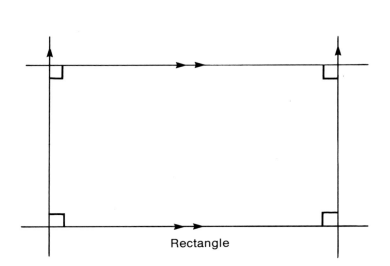

Rectangle

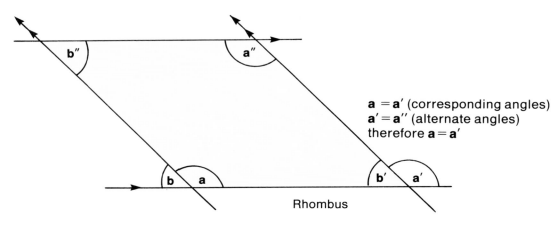

$a = a'$ (corresponding angles)
$a' = a''$ (alternate angles)
therefore $a = a'$

Rhombus

$b = b'$ (corresponding angles)
$b' = b''$ (alternate angles)
therefore $b = b''$

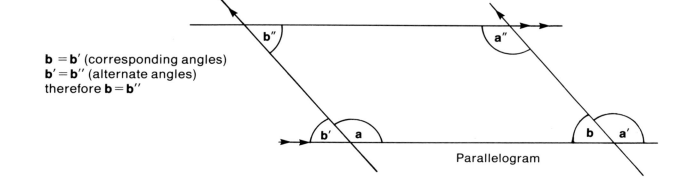

Parallelogram

Get in the Frame

Copy these figures exactly and cut them out carefully. Only cut out the shape, not the frame.

52

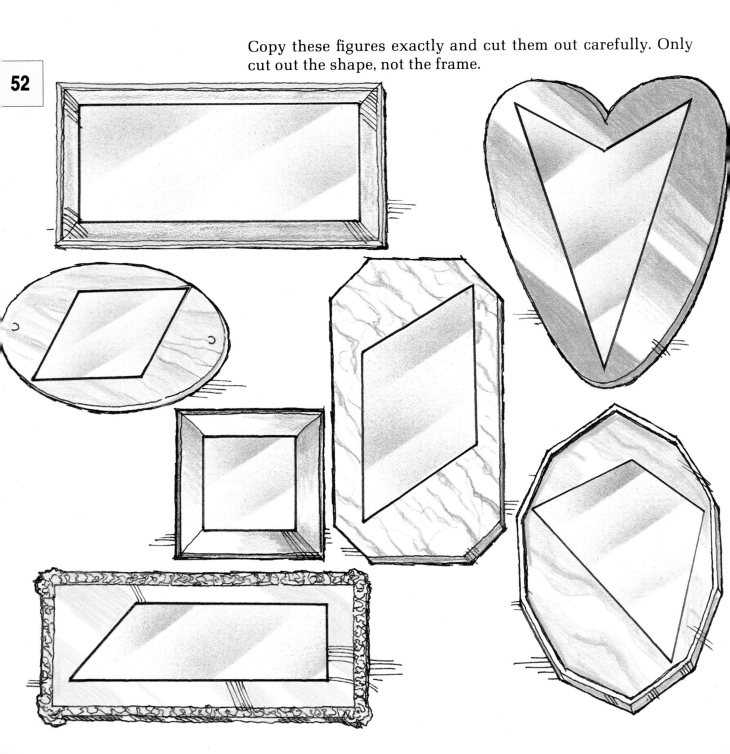

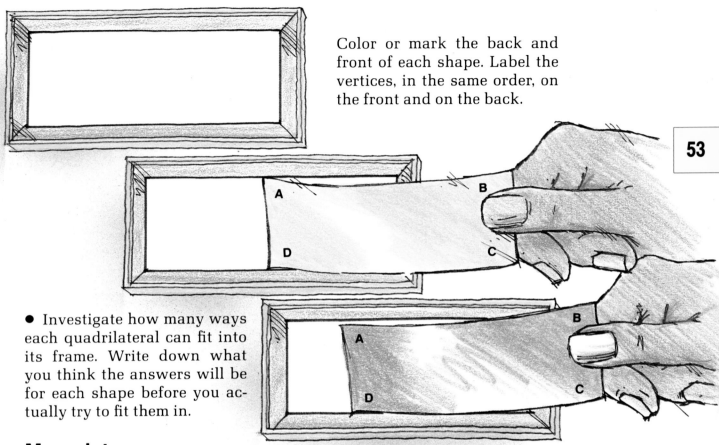

Color or mark the back and front of each shape. Label the vertices, in the same order, on the front and on the back.

● Investigate how many ways each quadrilateral can fit into its frame. Write down what you think the answers will be for each shape before you actually try to fit them in.

More dots

● Make five rows of five columns of dots. Start where you wish and join two dots to make the side of a square. What is the greatest number of squares you can make without lifting your pencil from the paper or going over any line twice?

Target – 10 squares.

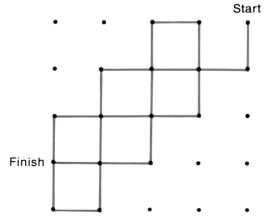

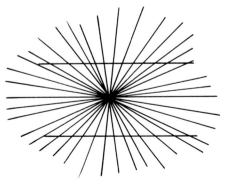

Are these lines parallel?

Shape Up

On scrap paper draw a circle with a **diameter** of about 5″. Keep the compass set at $2\frac{1}{2}$ and mark off around the circumference to draw a regular hexagon.

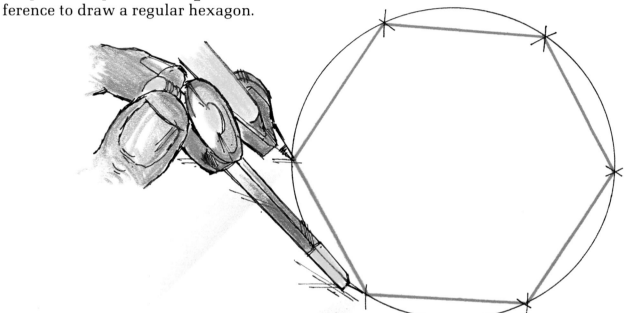

Make several copies of the hexagon. Investigate how many ways you can find of cutting it up so that the pieces form a rectangle.

Here is one example to get you started.

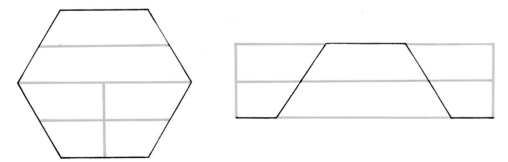

● What is the least number of pieces you need to cut?

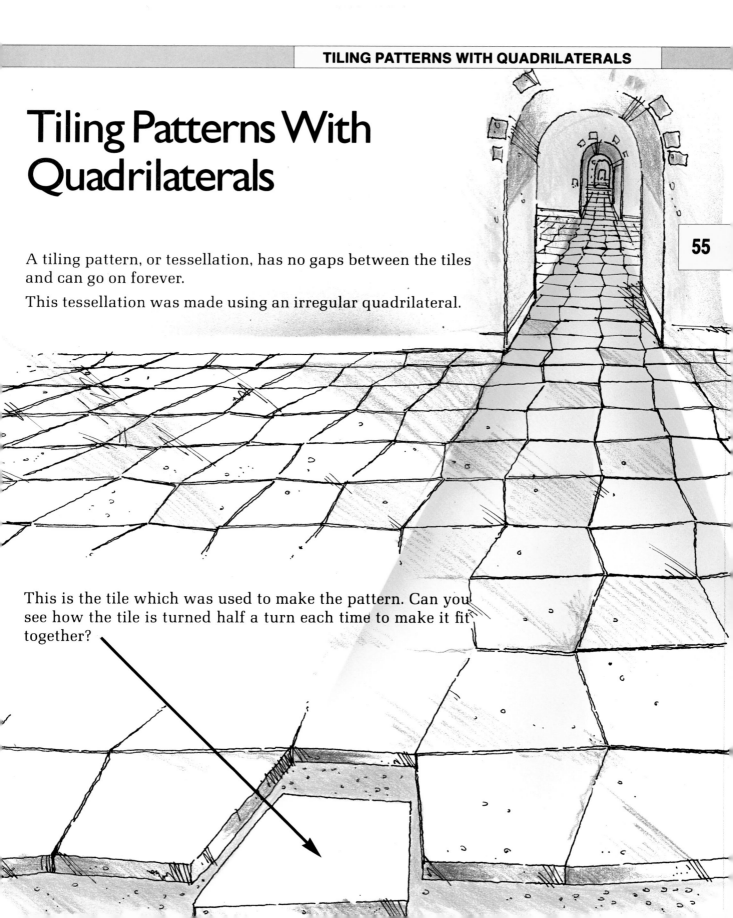

Tiling Patterns With Quadrilaterals

A tiling pattern, or tessellation, has no gaps between the tiles and can go on forever.

This tessellation was made using an irregular quadrilateral.

This is the tile which was used to make the pattern. Can you see how the tile is turned half a turn each time to make it fit together?

56

◇ Cut a quadrilateral tile out of cardboard and experiment with your own tiling pattern. You will probably find it helps to see the pattern building up if you label the four angles of the tile.

Instant parallelogram tiling patterns

You need tracing paper or a sheet of clear plastic. With a ruler, draw a series of parallel lines on a sheet of paper. On tracing paper, draw another series of parallel lines. Place the tracing paper over the paper so that all the lines are parallel. Rotate the tracing paper slowly and watch what happens.

Experiment with tiling patterns with other quadrilaterals. Some very attractive ones can be made with kites and arrowheads. If you look around, you will find many examples of quadrilateral tessellations on fabrics and furnishings.

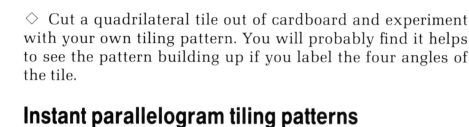

Rigid and Floppy Frameworks

The garden trellis, used to support climbing plants, is an example of a lattice of rhombuses. When you buy it, it is pushed together as a series of parallel lines. It can be stretched open when you put it up and made to fit a variety of lengths of fencing. This is because quadrilaterals are floppy, not rigid shapes.

◇ You can demonstrate the difference between a rigid and a floppy framework very simply. Cut seven lengths of drinking straws, wood or cardboard. Join the ends of three of the pieces to each other by binding with rubber bands or string. This forms a triangle. Join the remaining four pieces to make a quadrilateral.

57

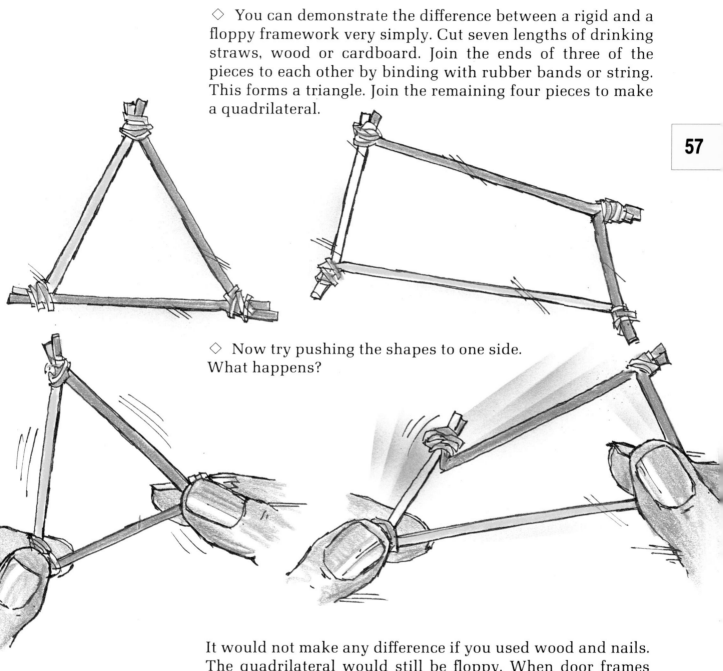

◇ Now try pushing the shapes to one side. What happens?

It would not make any difference if you used wood and nails. The quadrilateral would still be floppy. When door frames are delivered, they have cross pieces on the corners. These form triangles, which keep the frame rigid and in the correct shape until it is fitted into the house. Then the cross pieces can be removed.

Perimeters of Rectangles

The **perimeter** of a shape is the distance around the edge of it.

58

● What are the perimeters of these shapes?

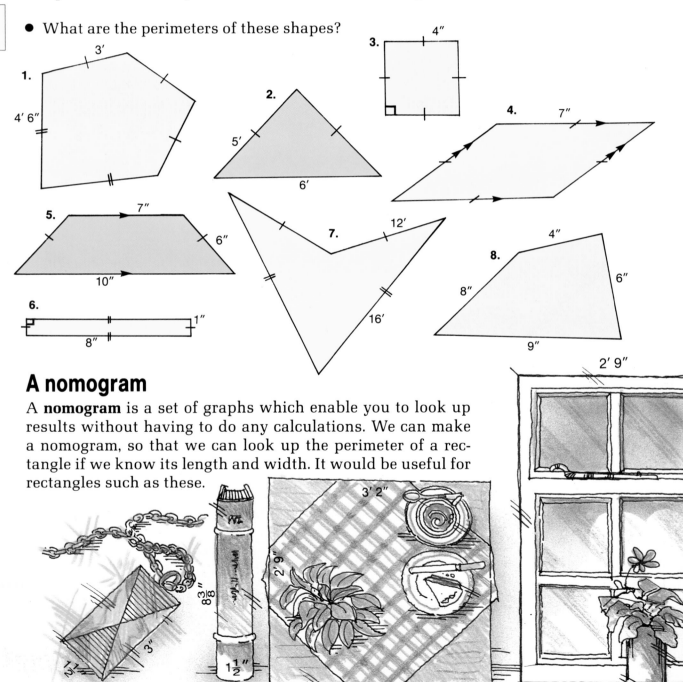

A nomogram

A **nomogram** is a set of graphs which enable you to look up results without having to do any calculations. We can make a nomogram, so that we can look up the perimeter of a rectangle if we know its length and width. It would be useful for rectangles such as these.

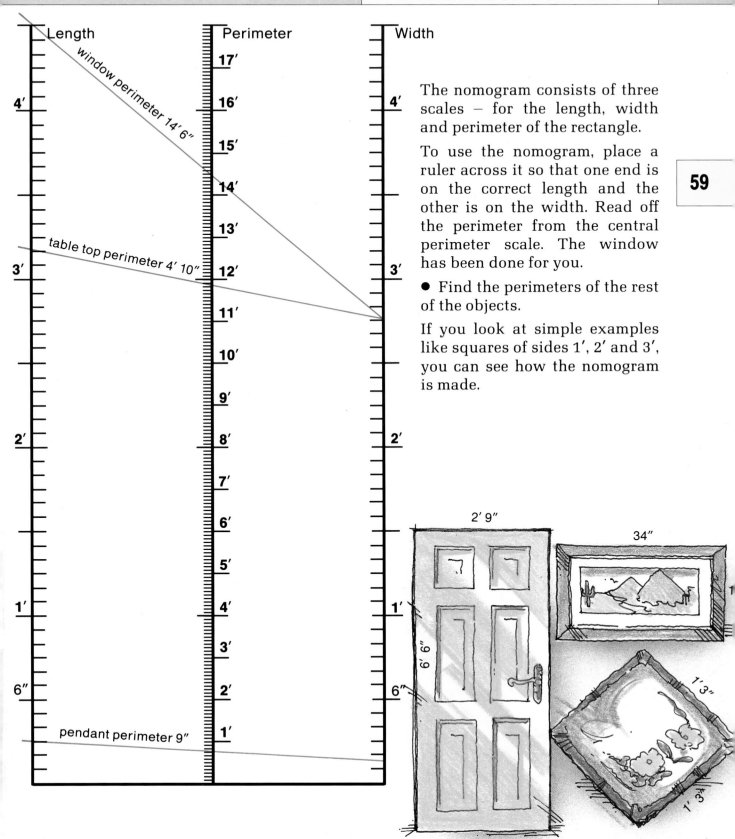

Length

Perimeter

Width

window perimeter 14' 6"

table top perimeter 4' 10"

pendant perimeter 9"

The nomogram consists of three scales – for the length, width and perimeter of the rectangle.

To use the nomogram, place a ruler across it so that one end is on the correct length and the other is on the width. Read off the perimeter from the central perimeter scale. The window has been done for you.

● Find the perimeters of the rest of the objects.

If you look at simple examples like squares of sides 1', 2' and 3', you can see how the nomogram is made.

59

2' 9"

34"

6' 6"

1' 3"

1' 3"

Investigating Fibonacci Rectangles

60

You need graph paper.

1. Draw a square with sides one unit long.

2. On one side of it, join another square one unit long. This makes a rectangle 2 × 1.

3. Draw a square on the long side of the rectangle. This makes a rectangle 3 × 2.

4. Draw a square on the long side of the new rectangle. This gives you a rectangle 5 × 3.

5. Draw the next square. You should get a rectangle like this. Look at the pattern of rectangles which is building up.

1 × 1   2 × 1   3 × 2   5 × 3   8 × 5

◇ What size do you predict the next rectangle will be?
◇ Draw it to see if you were right. The same pattern is building up in the lengths and in the widths of the rectangle.

● How does the pattern work?

An Italian, Leonardo Fibonacci of Pisa, was fascinated by this pattern nearly eight hundred years ago. It is often called the Fibonacci sequence, in honor of the work he did on it. You will probably come across it in many other contexts.

Rectangles which fit into the Fibonacci pattern are usually considered to be a pleasing shape by most people. This knowledge was used by the ancient Greeks in their beautifully proportioned buildings, such as the Parthenon.

You can carry out a survey to see whether this is true. Draw about ten rectangles, of which two are "Fibonacci" rectangles. Show them to people and ask them which rectangle is most pleasing to them. Record your results and then see if there are any clear favorites. You need to ask at least a dozen people.

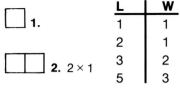
1.

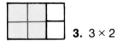
2. 2 × 1

L	W
1	1
2	1
3	2
5	3

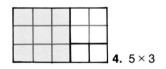
3. 3 × 2

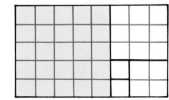
4. 5 × 3

5. 8 ×

Glossary

adjacent adjacent sides are next to each other.

arrowhead symmetrical quadrilateral, with one pair of equal angles and two pairs of equal sides, which looks like its name.

bisect cut in half. You can bisect a line or an angle.

closed shape a closed shape is one with no gaps between the lines which form its outside edges.

congruent if two shapes are congruent, they are the same size and shape. One will fit exactly on top of the other.

diagonal a straight line joining two vertices which are not adjacent.

diameter the distance across a circle from one point on the circumference to another, passing through the center.

equidistant at the same distance from.

horizontal a line perpendicular to a vertical line. The horizon is really slightly curved, but sometimes it looks like a horizontal line.

intersect lines intersect at the point at which they cross.

irregular not having equal sides and equal angles.

kite symmetrical quadrilateral, with two pairs of equal sides and one pair of equal angles, which looks like its name.

parallel parallel lines always remain the same distance apart, like railroad tracks.

parallelogram a quadrilateral with two pairs of parallel sides.

perimeter the distance around the edges of a shape.

perpendicular two lines are perpendicular when they meet at a right angle.

rectangle a parallelogram with right angles.

rhombus a parallelogram with all sides equal.

right angle a quarter turn; an angle of 90 degrees.

square a rectangle with equal sides.

trapezoid a quadrilateral with one pair of parallel sides.

vertex the point where sides meet. Any quadrilateral has four vertices.

vertical when you let a heavy object hang down on a string in your hand, the string is vertical. A vertical line is perpendicular to a horizontal line.

Answers

Page 7
See page 8

Page 9
See page 14.

Page 11
Opposite sides of a parallelogram are equal in length.

Page 14
See page 16.

Page 15

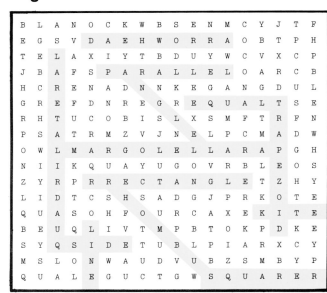

Page 17
See page 40

Page 18
See page 22

Page 19
The deliberate mistake is that one of the shapes labeled "irregular" is a trapezoid.

Page 20
See pages 22-23.

Page 21
See page 40.

Page 23

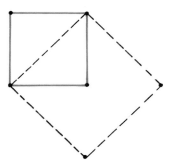

Page 26
See page 33.

Page 27
See page 33.

Page 30
See pages 33-5.

Page 31
See pages 36.

Page 32
See pages 36-37.

Page 38
See page 43.

Page 42

	Do the diagonals bisect each other?	Are the diagonals equal?	Are the diagonals perpendicular to each other?	Do the diagonals bisect the angles at the vertices?
Square	Yes	Yes	Yes	**Yes**
Rectangle	Yes	Yes	No	**No**
Parallelogram	Yes	No	No	**No**
Rhombus	Yes	No	Yes	**Yes**
Kite	No - only one	No	Yes	**No - only one pa**
Arrowhead	No - only one	No	Yes	**No - only one pa**
Trapezium (not isosceles)	No	No	No	**No**

Page 43

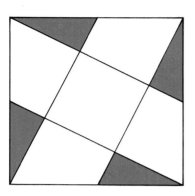

START

STOP

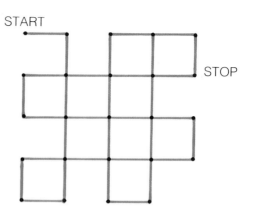

This is one way of scoring 10 squares. There are others you may have found.

Page 44

The angle at the point where the four pieces meet is 360°.

Page 45

The sum of the angle of any quadrilateral is 360°.

a = 78° **b** = 205° **c** = 147° **d** = 68° **e** = 94°
= 66° **g** = 90° **h** = 286° **i** = 124° **j** = 52°

Page 46

See page 50.

Page 47

Table answers – see page 50.

The trapezoid is a parallelogram.

What am I? **1.** A kite **2.** A rhombus

Page 49 and 50

Vertically opposite angles are equal, alternate angles are equal and corresponding angles are equal.

Page 53

The rectangle, 4 ways

The parallelogram, 2 ways

The arrowhead, 2 ways

The trapezoid, 1 way

The square, 8 ways

The rhombus, 4 ways

The irregular quadrilateral, 1 way.

Page 54

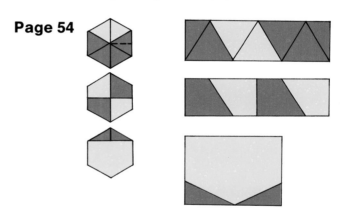

The least number of pieces is three.

Page 58

1. 18′ **2.** 16′ **3.** 16″ **4.** 28″ **5.** 29″ **6.** 18″ **7.** 56′
8. 27″

Page 59

Window 14′6″ Spine of book 19¾″ Door 18′6″ Cushion 5′ Picture frame 102″ Table top 11′10″ Pendant 9″

Page 60

After the second row the pattern works, in both columns, by adding each number to the one before.

L	W
1	1
2	1
=3	2
5	3
8	5
13	8 =

Index